Stop Yelling and Love Me More, Please Mom Workbook

Jennifer N. Smith

D1527614

Introduction

Being a parent is one of the hardest jobs in the world; being a good parent is harder than that. There's no guidebook that can help you become the parent that you want to be for your child and yes, I am writing that in the Introduction of a parenting guidebook. Because as much as I've tried to be helpful in this workbook, you have to do most of the work yourself.

Prior to this workbook, I have another book with the same title: "Stop Yelling and Love Me More, Please Mom!" That book of mine was about positive parenting, i.e. how to be a good parent to the child you love so much and to discipline them without having to yell and bark orders to them, and what to do when they don't listen.

As we all know, children have a hard time listening when we are yelling at them. Also, most of the time, we are yelling not because we are trying to make them listen, but because we are frustrated, angry and let's admit it – **helpless!** Shouting never helps the situation. We know that, the kids know that, everyone in the universe knows that. But we still shout.

My first book was not just about not yelling, but about trying to understand your child through the different stages of their life. This book is actually a workbook that complements my first book; the chapters complement each other. Everything I've discussed in each of the chapters of my first book, I've explained more in this book, and added little exercises or tips that you can try or follow. The first book, as a standalone, is fine, as is this book, but together, they can help you (hopefully) to be the kind of parent that you want to be.

So, good luck!

Chapter 1: Dealing with a Rough Day

I

When you are a mom, it's a given that your days are going to be hectic. Whether you are a stay-at-home parent or a working one, whether your children go to high-school or pre-school, your mornings – and any time of the day when the kids are at home - are going to be chaotic, and there's no way to avoid that. To be honest, anything to do with children is unpredictable. They can be in any mood any time of the day, and it is usually the mom's duty to manage the environment (Yes, manage; not control). You might have absolute control over everything at work, or any other aspect of your life, but when it comes to your children, it is not always going to be possible. You have to expect chaos and confusion with parenting.

So, first things first.

You need to make sure your day doesn't start that way! Weekday mornings can be hectic with or without you having to leave for work as well. What you need to do is to make sure your mornings start the way YOU want them to start, not the way your children do.

Start your Day your Own Way

The first mistake that you are making early in the day is to wake up in a house of chaos, where everyone is in a hurry, everyone is frantic, and everyone wants something for you. Your brain goes into overdrive the moment that it wakes up. From blissful sleep, you are flung into action without a moment's notice. No wonder you become agitated and temperamental, ready to lose your mind over the simplest matters.

Your mornings should always be your own. The simplest way to make that happen is to wake up half an hour or so earlier than everybody else. This would mean less sleep for you, yes, when you are already probably sleep deprived. But this would also mean that you are getting 30 precious minutes for yourself.

These 30 minutes doesn't have to mean something monumental for you. You don't have to do something very important to mark these minutes. You can just go on lying down in the bed making plans for the rest of the day, or you could read the papers. Have a cup of coffee in leisure in the silence of your kitchen, or read a few pages of the book you've been trying to finish forever. Or, you can start your morning routine a little earlier than normal, take your time getting ready or making breakfast.

Simply by waking up a little earlier, you are starting the day on your own terms. If you are too busy to make time for yourself throughout the day, this is the perfect way for you to do so. Mothers are usually on their toes all day, and exhausted by bedtime, too tired to make any time for their own lives. If you start the day earlier than the rest of your household, or earlier than your routine demands you – you are gaining some precious minutes for yourself.

Besides, this way, you are not going to start the day harassed by the clock. If you wake up exactly when you were supposed to, every minute onwards is counted for. Make a mistake in one single step and you are off to a bad start of the day. Wake up earlier and you have time on your hand; you will feel much better about the impending day when you've started it your own way.

Just a few minutes by yourself at the beginning of the day will put you in a much better mood than if you had woken up to a series of tasks and chores.

II

<u>When your mornings start in a bad way, it is really, really tough to keep your temper and not SHOUT.</u> This is usually what happens when you are out of time, out of options, and out of patience. If you have young children or teenagers, they can sometimes really get on your nerves. Screaming comes naturally in situations like this, but it doesn't really help the matters. When you start screaming at your children, they will stop listening to you either because you scare them or because they have gotten used to you yelling all the time.

In either case, yelling never works. It makes matters worse and it is definitely the time to stop yelling at your kids.

How NOT to Scream at your children?

Imagine that you have just spend a quiet moment at home, and then you suddenly realize: *it's been too quiet*. You rush around the house trying to locate your 3-year old and find her using your favorite lipstick as a crayon to draw on your very expensive handbag. You just know it's never going to come out!

Screaming comes naturally in such situations when you are feeling angry, frustrated and helpless at the same time. But screaming at your kids because they had made a mistake or been naughty will harm your relationship more than you can ever know. You might be able to scare them to do something or extract a *sorry* for them, or you might find a little bit of satisfaction in their tears, but they will start to fear you from that moment on.

It's hard NOT to scream sometimes, that's true! **But *it is possible.*** No one is asking you to act cool and patient all the time, because that is just not possible. Children, can really push you over the edge at times, without even meaning to. But as the adult here, you need to be the mature one to handle the situation well.

So, when the situation is so bad that screaming is the only way to release your pent-up anger and frustration, what do you do?

#1

You don't scream. Simple. **You just stop screaming, or you stop yourself from screaming any further.**

Automatically and instinctively, you might give a shout when you face something atrocious that your child has done or said, but that's it. That's absolutely IT. That's the only scream you are allowed. Your child might get startled after that first scream, but they probably won't be scared. The first shout will be instinctive and you can't stop that, but you can stop the ones afterwards.

#2

Instead of shouting insults and threats, just say, "Stop it!" Use a voice slightly higher than your normal one, but lower than when you are shouting. When you scream, your children will get scared and they might not even hear what you are trying to say. However, if you use a stern voice to say "Stop it!" or "Listen to me right now!" it might get their attention better. They might actually listen to you and stop doing whatever mischief they were up to.

#3

If you are not in too much of a hurry, take a few deep breathes. Inhale and exhale a few times, and give your brain the oxygen it needs to face the crisis at hand. Taking a few deep breathes will give you enough time to control yourself and to think things through. Spend a minute or two in silence so that you don't start screaming again. Come back to the situation only when you are confident that you are not going to yell at your children.

#4

However, just because you have constrained yourself from screaming, it doesn't automatically mean that you should back off and forgive them. They have still done something mischievous and wrong, either by intention or because they didn't know any better. You don't have to scream to discipline them. You just need to find a more effective way to get through to them.

Whatever they have done needs to be addressed. Get down to their eye level, hold them by the hand (tightly, but not roughly) and make your words count. **"DO. NOT. TOUCH. MOMMY'S. THINGS." Use a firm voice without raising it much.** Instead of using a lot of words, use only the important ones. Your message needs to be short and easy to understand. Without exactly screaming, make your words powerful. Repeat them if necessary, but don't change your tone.

#5

Take a moment to think about the whole thing. Did your child do something because they didn't know any better, or were they being mischievous intentionally? Did they do something they didn't know they shouldn't have, or did they disobey you on purpose?

If they had destroyed something without knowing it was fragile or expensive, you can't really be angry with them, can you? You can't assume they would instinctively **"know better"** because they won't. You can't scream at them when they've made a mistake unknowingly, and not actually been mischievous. If this is the case, **any yelling on your part would have been a mistake, and not what they deserve.**

Find out next...

Even if your children have been deliberately naughty, you need to find some other way to discipline them without screaming. Why? **Because shouting never helps.**

Yelling at your children can help you vent, but it is not the right way to be a parent. Whatever your child has done, being a parent means that you cannot scream at them or threaten them, physically hurt them or even spank them, or scare them into submission or insult their intelligence. They are the absolute wrong ways of parenting.

This is what we are going to discuss in the next chapter of this book: **the kind of parent you shouldn't be.** Not very long ago, there were only two parenting styles that were common in our society, and both of them have lost their credibility over the decades. It is now time to settle on a parenting style that is quite unlike the way our parents and grandparents were familiar with, a style that is more suited to the present.

Chapter 2: How to Not Raise a Bully or a Rebel

When we were growing up, there were two types of parents we could see among our family and friends: the ones who said "No" to everything, and the types who almost never said "No". Now, it's not very hard to imagine which type of parents we loved more in our childhood, is it? But the truth is, both parenting styles – the strict ones and the lenient ones – are bad for children.

We all learn parenting by watching our own parents and caregivers, or from the other parents we see around us: our grandparents, uncles and aunts, parents of our friends, and from households we are allowed into. It is the collective knowledge of our whole lives that we apply with our own children.

Do you remember thinking "I am never going to do that to my kids!" when growing up when you've watched an extremely frustrated mother hit her child? Or, have you ever thought "That's how I want to be with my daughter," when you've seen a lovely mother-daughter moment. This is exactly how each and every individual learn and decide on a parenting style to later apply in their lives. We learn to be a parent not from parenting books or college education, but from our experiences and our expectations.

I

What kind of a Parent Are You?

Now, there were, in the past, two main styles of parenting that we could see, with a little variety in each case: **"strict" parenting and "permissive" parenting**. The "Strict" parenting style is comparatively old-fashioned compared to "permissive" parenting, and quite outdated. But the "permissive" parenting style is also on its way to become extinct quite soon.

These parents believe in heavy discipline, limitations and boundaries. There are some parents who still think spanking and starving their children help shape them better in their lives. Remember the ridiculous old saying "Children should be seen and not heard"? The "strict" parents are the type who still believe in this saying.

"Permissive" parents, on the other hand, doesn't believe in saying "no". They don't believe in boundaries or limitations either; they give in to their children's wishes as soon as they are made. "Permissive" parents think that doing so will make their children feel loved and appreciated at all times, and they will grow up as the individual they were meant to be.

Since these are the parenting styles we are most accustomed to seeing, we grow up to be either one of these two types of parents, or a variation of these two. While a style of parenting that is a mixture of these two are acceptable, neither "Strict" nor "permissive" parenting is very healthy for a child.

If you are any one of these two parent types, know that you are either going to raise a child who is submissive, have low self-esteem and a liar, or a child who has eventually grown up as a spoiled brat who thinks all their demands must be met at once. Neither extremity is very welcome in this word, are they?

No, they are not. **We neither want a spoilt child nor one with no confidence.** To raise a mentally and emotionally healthy child, you need to settle on a very different parenting style that is neither extreme nor very indulgent. We are going to discuss this in the next chapter of this book.

For now, it is important to know the special traits of "strict" and "permissive" parenting, to know exactly what to avoid doing.

II

How not to be a "Strict" Parent

These are some of the things that "strict" parents do or say that is extremely harmful for your child's mental and emotional development.

- Spanking or hitting is always a big "NO"! Under no circumstances should parents hit or physically abuse their children, or even scare them with physical threats.

- Yelling or screaming when they have made a mistake doesn't help either. Screaming regularly at your children will eventually stop them from paying any attention to you, or make them fear you.

- Not listening to their side of the story after they've done something can be harmful.

Children should at least be given a chance to explain their actions before you punish them. Otherwise, they will feel unheard and invisible.

- Controlling every little aspect of their life is equally frustrating. Some parents criticize and regulate every move their children make and everything they say, believing they are only trying to better their kids. In truth, children who find themselves continuously under scrutiny will have absolutely no self-confidence or self-esteem.

- Denying something that every other child has access to or owns can make your child depressed. If you are intentionally denying something that your children rightfully want - not for financial reasons, but simply because you can, it's going to break their hearts.

- Some parents have a very bad habit of negatively comparing their children with others, often in front of the children themselves and other people. This is one of the worst things that parents can do for their children, as the constant comparisons can depress them and lower their self-esteem.

- Physical affection, occasional hugs and kisses, silly games – these are all extremely important for children. If you are too impatient to indulge in these games or if you consider them a waste of time, as a strict parent do, you will lose the chance to bond with your children.

- While rules are good for children, too many rules can be stifling. Strict parents have a long list of rules in the house, with absolutely no exceptions under any circumstances, which can feel excess.

- Children need a little time off to have fun on their own. If you think yourself responsible for every second of their lives, you are being more of a jailor than a parent. Parents need to allow children some free time to find their own entertainment, rather than micro manage everything.

- Young children are not capable of making big decisions for themselves, but they need to be given small choices. Strict parents don't offer any choices to their children but make the decisions for them, even if it is simply a matter of choosing an ice-cream flavor.

- Strict parents are always concerned about not letting their children make any kind of mistakes, which is actually something against nature. Children are supposed to make mistakes, and then learn from them, but these types of parents don't let that happen.

- Parents who are extremely strict with their children have **absolutely zero tolerance level** for mistakes. As a result, in order to avoid the impending punishment for making a mistake, **they learn to lie.**

- Strict parents only care about the outcome of their children, and never the effort they put into the task. Since not all children are born with the same qualities, some of them may fall behind in their studies or sports, social skills or special talents. Instead of accepting their children as they are, strict parents only pressure them more to excel, even in subjects they are weak in or have no interest in.

- Since extremely strict parents are not very close to their children, they can never have a heart-to-heart intimate discussion about the sensitive sides of life, i.e. puberty and the physical changes during puberty, attraction to the other gender, having a crush on someone or about sex. Children often learn about these topics from other equally misinformed children and get confused.

More importantly, children are almost never comfortable with strict parents. They can't share any of the important parts of their lives with their parents, the people who are supposed to be the closest confidantes. In a strict household, laughter and jokes are rarely heard, and children feel lonely and invisible, born only to fulfil a goal rather than live their life.

III

How not to be a "Permissive" Parent

"Permissive" parents are completely opposite to "strict" parents, usually victims of strict parenting in their own childhood. People who have lived a hard and lonely life under the critical observation of their strict parents tend to spoil their own children with excessive love and no discipline. While their intentions may be good, some of the parenting steps that they take end up harming their children in the long run.

These are the features you can find in "permissive" parent that need to be avoided.

- **Permissive parents don't believe in rules and structures.** They believe that rules and routines would hamper their children's natural growth when in truth, children crave some structure in their life. While strict parents overdo rules and regulations, permissive parents let their children do anything they want to do. This makes it harder for most children to adjust to school or social situations where decorum should be maintained.

- Just like permissive parents don't believe in rules, they don't believe in disciplining their children either. When their children make a mistake or disobey them intentionally, these parents usually let the whole matter pass by saying "Kids will be kids". This teaches children that they can get away with anything, even in the real world.

- It's the children in a permissive household who makes the rules, not the parents. If they want to stay awake past midnight, they are allowed to; if they want ice cream for breakfast, they are usually given what they want. While this kind of indulgence is acceptable sometimes as a treat, children who makes the rules in their homes usually leads an imbalanced life later.

- **Permissive parents buy their children whatever they want, whenever they want it.** Their demands are fulfilled the moment they voice it, even when they are illogical. As a result, they neither have any value for their belongings, neither any respect for their parents' financial situations. Later, these children grow up irresponsible about money.

- Parents who are permissive prefer to avoid conflict with their children rather than face them, which makes them say "yes" to anything their children ask of them. Most of the time what toddlers and teenagers want to do isn't good for their own health or development, but they still get to do what they want to because their parents aren't comfortable with conflict and argument.

- Teenage is a particularly trying time for parents. Teenagers are, by default, filled with loathing against their parents, and there is almost no way to avoid that. Permissive parents hate that their teenage children dislike them and in order to make themselves seem "cool" or to make their children like them, they allow everything. This includes everything that can be harmful to their children, but permissive parents are more concerned with keeping a good relationship.

- Children who have a lot of belongings easily get tired of what they have, and demand more. The easiest solution for parents is to give them the gift of technology when they are too young for it. Too many gadgets at a very young age is not right for any children, and it hampers their physical and mental development.

- **As a mean of good behavior, permissive parents bribe their children with promises of toys, unhealthy food or gifts.** While acceptable on special occasions, bribery isn't a good way to make sure your children behave. Growing up, these children will not know the correct way to behave unless a bribe is offered.

- Children growing up in a permissive family will negotiate every step of the way. Since their parents are not very strict and the rules are flexible, children learn to negotiate to get everything their way.

- If ever permissive parents try to stand their ground on a matter, the children react by lashing out physically. They may try to hurt themselves when they don't get what they want, break their belongings, or even hit their parents back.

Most importantly, children from a permissive family are not aware of any limits they need to maintain. They are used to get what they want, anytime and anywhere, without working or waiting for it. **These children are mostly known as "spoilt brats" to the outside world because their parents have spoiled them with too much freedom and not enough limitations.**

Neither "Strict" nor "Permissive" parenting is very good for your children's overall well-being. When it comes to parenting, you cannot be too harsh or too laidback, but opt for a more peaceful option in between.

Your children are your dearest family members, but that does not mean you should spoil them with too much affection. On the other hand, just because it is your responsibility to raise them properly, it doesn't mean that you should be extremely strict with your children.

What is the perfect parenting style, then? That's what we are going to know in the next chapter of this book.

Chapter 3: Understanding Child Development Stages

When we have a baby, our first impulse is to shower it with love – more love and affection than we can manage. Our children are precious to us, and we love them more than we love our lives, and want to protect them from the rest of the world. Whether it is our first child or our fifth, the emotion is always the same.

Unfortunately, love isn't the only gift we should reserve for them. As they grow up and start developing their own personalities, the tough job of disciplining them also falls on us. By disciplining our children, we are preparing them for the outside world where they'll need to not only survive, but thrive, without our assistance. We discipline them by teaching them the correct responses and emotions, by showing them the right path to choose, and by developing confidence and self-esteem in them.

Disciplining our children requires us to understand their development stage first. Just as we cannot expect a newborn to learn their alphabets, we cannot expect a toddler to make their own breakfast. We can put pressure on them, threaten them or teach them repeatedly, but they will learn only when they are ready to do so.

If you are not sure when your children are ready for proper discipline, read ahead. I have divided childhood into several sections and described what children at that age will be able to do.

Stage 1: Birth to 3 months

The first stage of your baby's life isn't for disciplining, but for showering love and attention. Although newborns aren't aware of most things that happen around them, they are aware of their own physical needs. Very young babies will cry to attract attention when they ae hungry or wet, cold or hot, or when they need some human touch.

During this stage, babies can't do much except:

- Smile, either in their sleep or when they have company;

- Look at bright colors and lights;

- Listen to sounds made around them;

- Start to reach; and

- Lift their hands to be held.

Stage 2: 4 months to 6 months

Subtle changes occur almost every day during this stage, changes only the parents or people close to the baby can identify. By this time, babies can:

- Laugh out loud;

- Discover their own hands and feet;

- Can remain seated if someone helps;

- Roll over;

- Grab for things and grasp them;

- Bounce while sitting down;

- Put things in their mouth;

- Cry when someone shouts;

- Locate whoever is talking or making a sound; and

- Make unintelligible noises.

Stage 3: 7 months to 12 months

These 6 months are monumental in a child's life; they learn to stand and walk, or say their first words. This is the time babies start to be aware of the world around them, and notice other people beside their parents and regular caregivers. Within these 6 months, children learn to:

- Take their first steps and then walk properly;

- Say their first words;

- Enjoy and dance to music and nursery rhymes;

- Know their own name and respond to someone calling;

- Wave goodbye;

- Distinguish family members from strangers;

- Play and understand "Pat-a-cake" and "Peek-a-boo";

- Recognize their own toys;

- Reach for anything unfamiliar and interesting; and

- Try or refuse food they see other people eating.

It is from their first year that children will be able to properly respond to disciplinary measures. They will be able to remember what their parents deemed as dangerous or "Ouch!", or what they are not allowed to touch.

Stage 4: 12 months to 18 months

By the time your children pass their first birthday, they will become more and more aware of their own selves as well as their surroundings. They will slowly start to respond to instructions given by you or other people close to them. They'll also be able to:

- Start making two-word sentences
- Run;
- Listen to and nod to stories;
- Know around 50 words;
- Play with interactive toys;
- Watch television;
- Show signs of love for people close to them;
- Show when they want a hug or a kiss; etc.
- Look at bright colors;
- Eat with their own hands; etc.

Stage 4: 18 months to 24 months

This is the time to properly start implementing discipline and routine with your children, although

they will take a long time and numerous trials to understand them. This is when parents need to tell children to not touch anything dangerous, not to hit or bite someone, or throw things, or spit. Of course, they will still do what you ask them not to, especially if they find it funny, but from 18 months onwards, parents should definitely start setting limits.

After 18 months, toddlers should be taught:

- To eat properly with their finger;
- To try to use a spoon and/or fork;
- To pick up their toys and put it back in the toy chest/cupboard;
- To wear their own clothes (or at least, try to);
- To share toys with siblings and other children;
- To fall asleep on their own;
- To indicate when they need to use the toilet;
- To sit at the table with the grown-ups;
- To look at books and point at familiar pictures;
- To go and fetch an object they are familiar with;
- To understand when someone says "No!" and "Don't touch!";
- To understand when their parents are taking away a toy for being naughty;
- To use their "inside voice" when you have company or when out;
- To understand simple instructions; etc.

Stage 5: 2 to 3 years

If you don't seriously start to discipline your children at this stage, it will be too late. From when they are 2 years old, children need a lot of affection, but they also need limitations. Too much affection and freedom will turn you into a permissive parent, and your child will make the rules in the house; too much limitations will mean they would grow distant from you. **Parenting a two-year old means that you would have to be loving and caring, and also strict when needed.**

From when your children are two years old, they should:

- Be able to entertain themselves alone for some time;

- Have a strict bed time;

- Take a single nap during the day;

- Use a spoon or a fork by themselves;

- Choose their own toys to play with;

- Put their toys back to where they belong;

- Turn pages in a book properly;

- Help you around the house in simple chores, i.e. folding clothes;

- Brush their teeth with help;

- Wear their clothes by themselves (even if they are backwards);

- Be able to choose between two options;

- Understand when a parent is angry at them;

- Show too much interest in the TV and handheld gadgets;

- Try to imitate what their parents are doing, etc.

Stage 6: 3 to 5 years

These days, children grow up very fast. By the time they are 4 years old, they are quite the adult. From 3 to 5, children develop their own personalities and choices. They make friends at school and learn from them; they might even seem completely different to the child you raised.

Between 3 to 5 years of age, children should be taught:

- Not to lie (they might sometimes, so there's nothing to worry about);

- To always confess if they had made a mistake or broken something;

- To tell you everything that has happened to them;

- To complete their morning and night ritual by themselves;

- To fall asleep by themselves;

- To limit their screen time to only two hours a day;

- To make their own bed (at the best of their abilities);

- Tidy up their toys, books and other belonging;

- Put on their own shoes;

- Eat their own meals;

- Comb their own hair (but not tie them);

- The difference between "good touch" and "bad touch";

- To go to the toilet by themselves when needed;

- To drink water every now and then;

- To help you around the house;

- To not touch things that are restricted to them;

- To not use what is not theirs without asking permission;

- To complete one or two chores by themselves; etc.

Children will gradually learn all of these life skills by themselves; some a little earlier than others. A five-year old will not need much help from you to entertain themselves, but they will need to understand their limits. If you never punish them or chastise them for doing something they shouldn't have done, i.e. for using your belongings when you have asked them not to, for looking inside other people's bags, etc. they will not know their limitations.

Stage 7: 5 years and up

Five-year olds should know exactly what their limitations are, and how much freedom they are allowed in the house. As a parent, you can allow them the freedom to choose toys in a store, but they shouldn't be the one who determines whether to get one toy or ten. They can choose between coloring or playing, but they should know when it is time to finish their homework.

A five-year old could be the perfect companion for your household chores. This is a great age to teach them responsibilities, and to take care of themselves. They can help you around the house and keep their own things tidy, even help you in preparing food. By this age, they are mostly independent and have a life of their own. They'll make friends outside the family and want to spend time with them, which is something completely normal for children.

Boundaries and freedom should be both present in your parenting style when dealing with a five-year old. You need to be the one who makes the rules in the house, but your children should have the freedom to express their desires, as well. A five-year old is just like an adult with a personality of their own; they have their own goals and desires in life. Shutting them up completely isn't a good idea, neither is to let them do whatever they want.

It's all about the balance.

Chapter 4: Communicating with your Children

If you've read my other book, you must have seen the different steps of positive parenting I have described in the 4th chapter. Children as young as 3-years old can understand your words, as well as your body language, when you talk to them. If you were a parent who used to yell a lot at them but now want to change your style, it is very important to talk to them about this change. Without talking to them about it, a big change in their usually verbal parent would scare them or make them suspicious.

Not all parents are very comfortable with talking to their children; they can show affection and shower love on their children, but not talk to them one-on-one. This is usually because we don't usually know how to talk to children so that they'd understand properly, or because we don't know what words to use. But with children, what's more important than words are your gestures, tone and eyes. These are what matter to children more than mere words. If they don't understand your words, they'll understand from your tone.

Talking to Your Child About Change

The first talk that you need to have with your child will be about the changes in your parenting style. If you had been a strict parent prone to yelling, this sudden change in you will make your child suspicious. On the other hand, if you have never denied your children anything before, setting limitations will also make them suddenly loathe you for them. Before you make any kind of change, it is therefore important that you talk to them about it.

Any child would understand your language after they are 3 or 4 years old, but you have to explain the whole thing in words they'd understand.

Try this approach:

> "Remember how Mommy used to scream and shout a lot before? (wait for affirmation or a nod). You didn't like that, did you? (Wait) Mommy didn't like it either! But Mommy used to get so mad sometimes when you were being naughty. You know how you sometimes want to yell when you are angry? (wait) That's why Mommy used to yell at you so much.

> "I know you were scared of Mommy. Well, I am not going to yell anymore from now on. Will that make you happy? (wait for a nod) It'll make Mommy happy too. If you are a good boy or girl, Mommy won't have to yell at you anymore.

> "Mommy loves you a lot and Mommy always wants to be a good Mommy. Will you help me be a good Mommy? (wait for a reply). Mommy really wants to be good for you, so that we can have lots of fun together. Do you want to have fun with Mommy? Thank you, my love! I know we're going to have lots of fun together! "

For an older child, you can have a different kind of talk.

"Do you remember how I used to yell at your every time I was mad? Well, I have decided that I am not going to do that anymore. I don't want to be the kind of mother you are afraid of. Do you want to be afraid of me? (wait for an answer) And I don't want to be someone you can't be comfortable with.

"I am going to try and be a good Mother to you, but I need you to try and listen to me, too. I don't want to punish you every day. Do you like to be punished? (wait) I don't like it either. I promise I will not punish you or yell at you from now on if you can listen to me. Shall we do that? (wait) Do you want to try with me to be a good son or daughter? Do you think we can both do that? (wait for an affirmative answer). Good, I hope so too."

Or, you can be a little firm about the whole thing.

"We haven't had a good relationship these last few years/months/weeks/days, have we? You're growing up and you have ideas of your own. But I am your mother and I am responsible for you until you know better. I love you very much and I care about you a lot. Do you agree to this? (wait for an answer) I am going to make the rules here and you have to listen to what I say, until you are big enough to know better.

"I know I used to yell a lot in the past and I am sorry for that. I am trying to better myself as a parent, but it means that you have to help me as well. I cannot be a good Mother if you are not trying to be a good son/daughter. Can I? (wait) Can you be good for me? Do you want me to be a good Mother? Will you help me? Can we do this together? (wait) Thank you very much!"

The tone and the words that you choose will depend on your child's age and maturity level, but you need to be sincere in your words. You need to mean what you are saying if you want your words to hit home.

Talking to Your Child About Finding Solutions

As a parent, you can make all the decisions for your children, but they need to learn to do the same. As your child grows up, they gradually need to find the solutions to their own problems. Especially if your child has a sibling, they need to solve all the disagreements by themselves. You can guide them to find the solutions, but not interfere in every fight that is going to take place.

Solving their own problems at home will teach them responsibility. Just like you have decided not to scream at your children, they must learn to resolve their fights without resorting to yelling and fighting. You can try something like this:

> *"Good children always share their toys with their brothers and sisters. Your brother/sister loves you and he or she wants to play with your toy for a while. They'll give it back to you soon. Will you be a good brother/sister and let them play with it? You can share your toy and play together. Would you like that? (wait for a reply)*
>
> *"No! You don't want to share your toy? In that case, why don't we keep it hidden somewhere they can't find it, and we play with something else? We'll play with it later, you and me alone. Is that okay? Right now, take something else that you can share with your brother/sister."*

While sharing with their siblings is a positive sign, children shouldn't always be forced to share something they love, not even with their brothers and sisters. They shouldn't feel like they're the ones always making the sacrifice. Your child is allowed to be selfish once in a while, and you shouldn't always pressure them to do what's right.

Lecturing your child to be nice to their siblings won't always work. Children know they are supposed to love their brothers and sisters, and they do, but there will always be some kind of clash going on in a house with multiple children. You cannot force your children to be nice to each other always, but you can empathize with them.

Try talking like this:

> *"I know you are mad at your brother/sister right now, but I also know that you love them a lot. Yes, I know that you do. You love them because they also love you a lot. You are allowed to be angry at them, but that doesn't mean you don't love them anymore, does it? (wait for an answer)*
>
> *"Did you like it when I used to yell at you? I bet you didn't. Well, your brother/sister doesn't like it when you yell at them. They get scared of you. Do you want them to be afraid of you? I know you don't. If you are angry at your brother/sister, can we do something else except yell at them? Do you want to go play on your own for the moment? Why don't you go play with a favorite toy of yours for now? When you are not angry at your brother/sister anymore, we will all watch some cartoons together. Will that be all right?"*

Talking to Your Child About Reparation

Just like your child doesn't like it when you yell at them, you get hurt when they don't listen to you. Children don't usually understand that they have the power to hurt you; they are not aware that their actions can have an effect on others. By the time they are 4 or 5 years old, you should explain to your children that what they say and do can hurt other people, and that they are responsible for making the necessary amendments.

Empathize with them like this:

> *"Do you remember when Mommy used to yell at you? Did you like it when I yelled? (wait for an answer). No, I know you didn't. Mommy didn't like to scream either. Mommy knew it made you sad. Did you like Mommy when she yelled? Were you scared of her? (wait) Did you cry when Mommy yelled? Did it make you sad? (wait) I know it did. That's why Mommy doesn't yell now. Do I shout at you anymore? Do you like it now that I don't yell at you?*

> *"Do you know what makes Mommy sad? Mommy becomes sad when you don't listen to her. Do you want Mommy to become sad? (wait for an answer). I know you don't want me to be sad, because I know you love me a lot. Mommy loves you a lot too, and it makes Mommy sad when you are rude to her. Mommy gets hurt when you talk rudely to her. Do you want to hurt Mommy? (wait for answer) Of course you don't, love. That's because you are my good*

baby. Good babies don't hurt their Mommy, do they?"

Or, give them the chance to make amends to their own behavior like this:

"Do you know that your sister/brother loves you very much? Do you know this? (wait for an answer) I know that you love them a lot too. You might be feeling angry right now, but I know you love them. I know that you love me a lot, too, don't you? How did you feel when I used to yell at you a lot? I bet you felt really sad, didn't you? Because you loved me a lot, it hurt when I yelled and called you bad. Didn't it? (wait)

"Don't you think your brother/sister is feeling very sad right now? They love you but you yelled at them. Didn't that hurt them? Do you think they are sad right now? (wait) Are you feeling sad because you made them unhappy? Do you want to do something nice for them? (wait for a moment) Do you think a sorry and a hug would make them happy? Do you want to do that right now? (wait for answer)

"Are you still angry at them? Do you want a few more minutes? That's fine. You can go find your brother/sister when you are no longer angry, and then you are going to give them a hug and say you are sorry. Does that sound good to you? Thanks, honey! I know you are a good boy/girl."

Teach them to Apologize

Your child isn't going to transform overnight into an obedient one as soon as you decide to change your parenting style, no. They'll need time to adjust to these new rules and regulations (or the lack of), and they will mess up in the meantime. Your children will need to learn how to apologize properly for any kind of mistakes that they make, or any rude behavior – to you, to their siblings or to someone else.

Telling them to "Apologize!" doesn't always work; if they do apologize after your command, it will be a half-hearted one at the best. Apologies need to be heartfelt, not forced. As the parent in the scenario, you need to "show" them how to apologize, not just order them to.

Suppose your child has been rude to a classmate, and now needs to say sorry. This is how you should probably deal with the matter:

"I know you didn't mean to be rude to your friends, because you are friends, aren't you? You go to the same school and sit in the same class, and you are friends. Friends aren't rude to each other, are they? I know you must be feeling bad inside because you didn't mean to be rude. Is that right? (wait for answer).

Of course you didn't. Because you are a good boy/girl. But since you've hurt your friends, don't you think you should say sorry? It's easy to say you are sorry, and you will feel so much

*better after you've said it. Go, say you're sorry,
and that you've been rude because you were
angry. Say you were wrong to be rude and that
you'll try your best to not be rude again in the
future, and that you want to be friends in the
future. Will you do that? (wait) That's like a
good boy/girl!"*

**Of course, that only works when your child was the one who had
been at fault. Be absolutely sure of the whole matter before you
ask your child to apologize.** You shouldn't force them to
apologize when they were not the ones at fault, but the other
party. Doing this will break their heart and their spirit, and they
will start to consider themselves to always be the faulty ones.
There's no need to apologize just to be polite when the blame lies
somewhere else; your child should only be asked to apologize
when they were to blame.

If you have never tried to talk to your children before like this,
don't be alarmed. Talking to children isn't very easy, but it's not
hard. The words themselves are important, but what's more
important is that you are sincere. Don't teach your children to do
something you would never do yourselves; don't tell them to be
considerate of other people's feelings when you don't think of
them. Don't teach them to apologize for their mistakes when
they've never seen you apologize for their mistakes. Don't teach
them not to yell at their siblings when you haven't stopped yelling
at them.

Children learn from your words and your lessons, but they also
learn more from your actions. Teach what you believe yourself,
and they will learn. Talk to them in their own language, but say
only what you mean.

Chapter 5: Stay Positive to be Positive

Whether you are planning on returning to work or becoming a stay-at-home mom, taking care of your child 24/7 can be a hard job. New-borns can sleep a lot through the day, but they also need constant attention and care; as the mother, you have to center your whole life around your child. Especially until your child reaches their first birthday, they are going to need their mothers – no one else, but the mothers – almost constantly. This kind of love and attention can actually make you seem stifled and trapped after a while.

If you are the only one stuck at home taking care of your child, the job will eventually lose its glamor after a while. In the initial few weeks or months, you might want to spend as much time as possible with your baby, but ultimately, you'll crave for a little break. You'll want to spend time with other people apart from your children for some adult conversation and carefree laughs. This doesn't mean that you have stopped loving your child, nor does this make you a bad mother; it just makes you a human being.

If you are feeling restless inside, you can't be a patient mother to your child. You need an occasional break to feel energized; you need to spend time with other people other than your children.

Taking a break from motherhood

We all need a break in our lives. When we work in an office or run a business, we can spend the evenings or the weekends hanging out with our friends, or taking off to the countryside. On the hours outside work, we are free to do anything we want with our time.

Unfortunately, motherhood doesn't give us weekends or evenings out. Nevertheless, mothers need to take some time out for their own mental health and happiness, even if it's an hour every week.

Here are some ways you can have a good time while still being a good mother to your child.

1. Take a Long Bath

This is a great way for mothers to relax without even leaving the home, if that's what you are worried about. When you have someone else in the house to take care of your baby in case of emergencies, you can take an hour-long bath with your favorite music or a book. But do this only when there is someone else in the house; otherwise, you would have to leave your leisurely bath halfway to tend to your crying baby.

2. Sleep on the Weekends

Another way that you can relax and still not worry about abandoning your baby is to have a sleepover by yourself on the weekends. Leave extensive instructions so that your partner or spouse can take care of their and the baby's breakfast, and let you sleep for as long as you want to. Arrange playdates too, if you can, so that you have most of the day free. Move over to the guest bedroom, turn off your phone and sleep like a log, secure in the knowledge that no one will wake you up unless you are ready.

3. Get a Mani-Pedi

If you truly want to relax, pop over to your local salon and let the person-in-charge give you a soothing mani-pedi. While you are at it, you can throw in a blow dry and a foot massage. It's hardly going to take an hour to do everything, but you are going to feel wonderful afterwards. Anyone can watch your sleeping baby for an hour while you are indulging yourself.

4. Grab a Coffee by Yourself

When all your other friends are mothers themselves or working girls, getting everyone together for a cup of coffee can become very hard. It takes half your energy just to plan a reunion with everyone. Instead, just leave your baby with your partner/spouse or a trusted caregiver, and head off to the local café. Order a cup of coffee with the most chocolaty cake you can find there, and read a new book for an hour or so.

5. Go Shopping ... For Groceries

If you always have too much to do and not enough time to do them, combine your chores with your "alone time". Even your grocery shopping could count as a "time-out" if you enjoy it. Buy something you'd ordinary not spend money on, munch on fattening snacks as you shop, buy more chocolate bars than is good for you, talk to the helpers at the meat section, spend unnecessary time deciding on a brand of detergent – you can do a lot of things at the local grocery shop for fun.

6. Go Window Shopping

Window shopping is much more fun than regular shopping. You can have a fun time at the mall without spending a lot of money, if that's a concern for you. Try on dozens of shoes because that always seem to cheer everyone up; try on seventeen dresses even if you end up buying a T-shirt. The people at the store won't mind if they see you enjoy yourself, and it could be a great way to spend a day with yourself.

7. Find a Mom Friend in the neighborhood

Whenever you feel like whining or venting, there's nothing better than a neighborhood Mom-friend. Your best friend won't understand your situation better than another mom, and it helps if they live in the same neighborhood. You can find them in the paediatrician's office, at the diaper aisle of the supermarket or in kid-friendly restaurants.

8. Catch a Movie

A movie is a 2-hour break by yourself when no one will disturb you. It doesn't matter what you watch as long as you get to do it alone. You can even take a nap if you don't like it, but a movie by yourself once a month (or more) is a great way to relax.

9. Go Running

The good thing with running is that you can do it at the break of dawn before the day starts for the rest of the family; besides, this is a great way to lose the pregnancy weight. Running in the morning will help you start the day in a great mood, and you'll get your exercises done and spend some time by yourself, as well.

10. Ask your Best Friend for a Sleepover

Sometimes, you simply need a binge-on-junk-food-and-gossip session with your best friend. Once or twice a month, ask your best friend to come over for a sleep over (or go over to her place), order at least four different pizzas, and gossip. Your partner or spouse can sacrifice their sleep for one night taking care of your child, or ask a grandparent to take the baby. Make sure you do this on the eve of a weekend, so that you can sleep late the next morning.

11.Start a Book Club

Even if you are not much into reading, start a book club with the other parents in your neighborhood and meet once a month. It will give you something to look forward to and plan for, and if you choose a big book, you'll always have something to do on your leisure moments. Moms usually love book clubs because it gives them a chance to think and talk about topics other than their children.

12. Stay Home

Sometimes, you simply need to stay home, alone, and not do anything. Nothing. Not a thing. Ask someone to take your child – preferably your partner or spouse – for a walk around the weekends, so that you can just sit on the couch, drink your coffee, and relax. You don't need to step out of your home for some rest; you can relax in the comfort of the home you have made for your family.

Sometimes, you simply need to be a woman and not a mom. These moments are, if very few in a mother's life, extremely necessary to remind you of the person you were before you had a child. You can love your child more than your own life, but you also need some time apart for yourself. It doesn't have to be days or even hours away from your child, but only a little time when you are a person, an individual with thoughts and ideas on your own.

Chapter 6: Managing Your Two-Year Old

Terrible two's – that's what it's called when your child reaches their second birthday. It's when your child starts becoming independent and wants to explore the world. They'll seem interested in everything and everyone they see, and their true interest would seem to lie outside the house. Mothers and fathers – not even siblings, but occasionally the grandparents – are a two-year-old's best friends rather than other children.

It's hard to discipline a two-year-old because they have just learned to discover the world. You'd want them to take a nap but they'd be too busy watching birds in the sky; you'd want them to eat healthy food but they've already had a taste for chocolate and they want more. But routine is extremely important for a two-year-old, as are some limitations. As the mother, you are not only supposed to be your child's best friend and supporter, but also their main keeper.

Routines for a Two-Year-Old

This is a sample daily routine of a two-year-old. Your household may force you to differ from this routine a little, but it should be something like it.

- 8.30AM: This is the time to get up, but if your child likes to sleep a little late, they should be allowed to sleep till 9.00AM at the most.

- 9.00AM/9.30AM: This is time for a hearty breakfast to start the day.

- 10.00AM: Playtime with Mommy.

- 11.30AM: Lunch within two hours of breakfast.

- 12.00PM: A little reading in a dark room to set the mood.

- 12.15PM: Naptime while Mommy rests and completes her chores.

- 3.30PM: Wake up in a good mood.

- 3.45PM: A little Snack, something they love.

- 4.00PM: A stroll in the park, a walk or playing in the yard.

- 5.00PM: Come home to play with your toys, or half an hour of television

- 6.30PM: Dinner.

- 7.00PM: A few cuddles, a little playtime.

- 7.30PM: Bath time.

- 8.00PM: Reading their favorite bedtime story/prayer.

- 8.15PM: Bedtime.

Boundaries for a Two-Year-Old

Your two-year-old is trying to grow up, but they are not mature enough to make decisions for themselves. They need boundaries; in fact, they crave discipline and limitations in their life even if they resist it. A two-year-old will try to do a lot of things they aren't old enough for, and they should neither be discouraged nor left to it.

These are the limitations you should set for your two-year-old.

1. Children these days discover the magic of televisions and tablets earlier than the previous generations, thanks to the HD screens we have. Two-year-olds love listening to and dancing to nursery rhymes, and it is occasionally okay to indulge them. Watching television is okay if it's done from a safe distance, and not for more than half an hour. Even doctors and child development specialists are okay with a little screen time if your child is watching age-appropriate content. A little television won't hurt your two-year-old unless they become addicted to it.

2. Bath times are important as well. Some children love taking baths every day, but other children hate bath times. You can forgo baths every now and then and settle for a sponge if your baby is too sleepy and tired. Baths make your baby relaxed and ready for bed, and they help settle your baby for bedtime. It's a routine that your baby needs to grow into as they mature.

3. Naps are also when children love to argue and resist. You can't blame them, can you? Who'd want to take a nap when there's a glorious day outside! But naps in the middle of the day are important, unless you want them to whine in the evenings. If they resist napping, a little reading in a dark and comfortable room can make them drowsy after lunch.

4. Your usually friendly child might suddenly turn hostile with someone in a matter of seconds. They might refuse to share their toys with other children or even refuse to say hello to one of your friends they know well. If that happens, there's no need to force them to do what you deem polite. Your child might be young but they are entitled to their own opinion sometimes. If your child is being hostile and unsocial but not exactly rude, let them be. Distract them with something else or leave them alone for some time.

5. Children as young as one-and-a-half-years-old can be potty trained, but they are not usually completely successful until they are two-and-a-half, or more. You have to get your children completely potty trained by the time they go to school or pre-school, so their 2nd birthday is a good time to start. By this time, children should be able to tell you around 60% of the time when they need to pee or poop, and be able to sit - with help and supervision - on a toilet seat or potty. They might still need a diaper at night or when going out, but they can stay for hours without one inside the house during the day.

6. Children of this age also start developing a sense of fashion. Girls might want to wear their princess dresses to a formal dinner and boys wouldn't get out of their Superman costume for dresses. While sometimes it's all right to indulge them, their comfort should always come first. If your two-year-old wants to go to the beach in a jacket or a sweater on a hot day, this is not something you should allow; neither if they refuse to wear warm clothes in winter.

7. There are other times when you just have to be adamant in your rules, no matter how much resistance you face, for the sake of your child's safety. A car seat is such an issue. Some children of this age refuse to sit in a car seat, but this is not something to negotiate with. Until they are old enough to manage, every child needs to be in a car seat, even if there is another adult in the back seat with an open lap.

Remember, that this is the age when children are actually testing their limits, to see just how far they can go. If you don't set their boundaries now, it will be too late. You don't need to punish your children for pushing their boundaries at this age, nor should you be too strict with them. **However, this is absolutely the right time to start showing them what you can and cannot do.**

Chapter 7: Making the Magic Years Special

Three to five – the time before they go off to school, make new friends and discover the world. They'll have a thousand questions but only you to ask them to. They'll feel curious about everything around them and want to know about them all. They'll try to understand logic in a way that's neither very mature nor very childlike; they'll behave like a grown up at times, yet be emotional like a baby. In short, it's a very confusing time for your child who is fast growing up.

Talking to your Growing Child

At this age, you can neither talk to them like they are babies, nor give them actual explanations of matters. You need to use words they understand, and at the same time, use new words so that they can gradually enhance their vocabulary. Since they still spend most of their time at home with you, their questions will be mostly about the situation at hand.

Here are a few sample answers that I have used myself, to some of the most common questions children could ask from ages three to five. Your child's questions could be different, but you'll get an idea of how to talk to them.

Q. Why does Daddy go away every day?
A. Daddy goes to *office,* honey, because he has a *job.* When he works in his office, he gets money. We use that money to buy your food, our clothes,

toys and books for you. We need money to *live,* so Daddy has to go work every day.

Q. Why won't you work?
A. Mommy works too, honey. Mommy *cooks* and *cleans* the house, and Mommy takes care of you all day long. Isn't Mommy busy all day? Daddy works in the office and Mommy works in the home.

Q. What will I do when I grow up?
A. You can do anything you want, my love. You can work in an office, or teach in a *school.* You can stay at home like Mommy do, or you can be a *pilot* and fly a plane. Or, you can drive a train! You like trains, don't you? Or, do you want to be a *doctor?* Do you know what a doctor does? Do you know the doctor we go to when you are sick? He gives you medicines and you feel better, don't you? Do you want to be a *doctor* like him?

Q. Where does the people in the TV come from?
A. Very far away. People use a *camera* to make *videos* of them, like we do with our phones. Then they send the videos to our television with *electricity* and long *wires,* so that we can watch them. Do you know what wires are? These are wires, these long black things, behind the television. Never touch them, because they'll give you a painful *shock.* Do you promise me never to touch them? Thank you!!

Q. Where does the sun go in the night?
A. The sun moves away at night, because it gets tired from giving us light and heat all day. The sun will come back the next morning again. It's still in the sky, but in another side and far away, so we can't see it anymore.

Q. Why does my brother look different from me?
A. Because your brother is a boy and you are a girl. Your bodies are different. Doesn't your daddy look different from me? That's because your daddy is a boy and I am a girl, that's why. But you and your brother are equal in every other way; only your bodies are different.

Q. How did the baby get inside your tummy? (Every pregnant woman has heard this at least twice!)
A. Mommy really wanted another baby, another brother or sister for you, and God gave it to us. But the baby was very small and couldn't live outside. So, Mommy is keeping the baby safe in her tummy

until the baby is ready to come out and play with you.

You get the gist, right? You are not exactly lying to them; neither are you making up stories for them. All you are doing is giving them the right answer, but in a language that they understand and not more than they need to know. You're also leaving them enough scope for imagination with your answers.

TV-free Play Ideas

Three- to five-year-olds love playing, but they lack the imagination to play by themselves. You need to supply them with the means to spend some quality TV-free time by themselves while you take care of your chores. Some of these playthings may require adult supervision, though.

Here's what you can try:

- Coloring, which can never go wrong.

- Playdoh.

- Get them a doctor set and a large doll that makes sounds.

- Age-appropriate puzzles.

- Lego (or age-appropriate Duplo).

Interactive hide-and-seek books.

Flash cards.

Look at hardboard picture books.

Playing with Mr. Potato head.

Kick a lightweight ball around, preferably outside.

Write gibberish or doodle in a notebook.

Play pretend with plush toys.

Play with an empty cardboard box, pretend it's a train or a rocket.

Make a fort with a bed sheet draped over the couches.

Family Activities with your Child

When the whole family is together, the most common pastime is often watching television. This leads to a lifetime of bad habit of sitting on the couch and staring at the TV, instead of spending our time together doing something more creative.

These are the activities you can do with your three to five-year-old, and with the whole family.

Coloring again; each family member can draw and color their favorite animals.

Finger paint.

Play in the yard with a hose or a sprinkler, Peppa-Pig style.

Make and play with some homemade playdoh.

Easy board games like Ludo, Snakes & Ladders, etc.

- Taking care of small indoor plants.

- Dressing up in your clothes.

- Bake cakes together or cook together.

- Dance together.

- Do an age appropriate puzzle together, or you can do one while they watch.

- Watch a cartoon movie together.

- Have a storytelling session.

- Play fun games like "Simon Says" and "Color Hunt".

- Play "Follow the Leader" with all the family members.

- Practice" yoga.

- Learn and practice with Flash Cards.

- Teach them to tell time by looking at a clock.

- Trace their first letters together.

Teach them to throw and catch.

Spend your evenings talking about your day.

Play with puppets and make up stories.

Play "Shop" with your own kitchen supplies.

You can make up more activities to do with your child at home. There's nothing that children love more than the company of their loved ones, much more than expensive toys or any other belongings. Children need quality time together with their family; they need to feel loved and wanted by the people who matter the most in their lives.

Before they go off to meet the rest of the world, children need the constant company of their family members in the comfort of their homes more than anything else.

Chapter 8: Connecting with your School-Aged Children

Your child is going to start changing very fast once they go off to school, which usually happens by the time they are five years old. Within six to eight, they are going to make friends and learn new things from them, most of them which you are probably not going to like. There will come a time, unfortunately, when they'll claim to love their teachers more than they love you, which is of course not true. In short, there is going to be a lot of things happening that you never planned for.

The main factor at this point is to not lose communication with your child. They'll be coming home with you at the end of the day, so you need to be there for them when they need you. Since they are not old enough to have a social life away from home yet, they still need you even though they seem more interested in their new friends.

Getting your Child to Talk

It is very important to ask the right questions to get your child talking. Your questions need to convey your genuine interest in their new life, something that "How was your day?" can't express anything. You can't really expect them to start talking if you don't know to ask the right questions.

Here are some questions you *can* ask:

- What made you *happy* in school today?

- So, what have your teacher been up to today?

- What's the most fun thing you learned today?

- What do you love to do in school?

- If you could do anything in school instead of study, what would you do?

- Which of your friends make you laugh the most?

- Did anyone do something funny at school today?

- Did the teacher say something funny today?

- Did someone do something nice for you today?

- Did you do something nice for someone today?

- Did you make someone smile at school today?

- Who bought the best lunch today?

- Did something different happen today?

- Who did you play with today?

- Which subject did you love the most today?

- Did you have trouble following any of the rules today?

- Did you make a new friend today?

- Did you help someone in their work today?

Questions like "How was your day?" would get you a non-committal "Fine" at best, or a "Nothing Different". But these questions are interesting, and your child will know specifically what to tell you about their day. These questions will also tell them that your interest in their day is genuine and that you are actually listening to them, **which is a big deal to them**.

Chores to Help Around at Home

If your child is old enough to go to school, they are also old enough to help you with some of the easy chores around the house. At this stage of life, they don't have to focus a lot on their studies; this time is more about social development than getting good grades. If they don't help you in cooking and cleaning, they should at least learn to clean up after themselves and keep their rooms tidy.

Here is a list of chores that a 6- to 8-year-old should be able to help you with. You might not feel comfortable with asking them to deal with everything in this list, but they should be, within this age limit, be able to do them.

- Make their own bed after they wake up;
- Prepare and check their school bag;
- Tidy their room before leaving;
- Select dirty clothes for washing;
- Carry clean clothes to their room;
- Fold their own clothes;
- Make a simple sandwich;
- Wash their own plate;
- Dry clean dishes;
- Dust and wipe top of furniture;
- Put away their books and toys;
- Help put away the groceries (with instruction);

- Water smaller plants;

- Get laundry (with supervision if it requires going outside);

- Help with small errands while cooking;

- Spot and pick up their belongings from all around the house;

- Answer the home phone (but not the door); etc.

The number of chores your child is ready for depends, of course, on their level of maturity. Not all children will show interest in folding clothes or gardening, but they will love assisting while cooking. Or, they might not show any kind of interest in the kitchen at all, but love taking care of all the little plants you have around the house. Their personalities will determine what kind of chores they'll help you more with in the future. This is not the time to put pressure on them about the type of chores you want them to do; let them choose as long as they learn to clean up after themselves.

For the time being, what's important is that children of this age start to understand their role and responsibility in the house as well as outside the house. As they start going to school, they need to also start taking responsibility for themselves at home. A healthy balance of school, studying, helping with chores and free time to play – they need all four in their lives.

At this age, children should only "start" to learn their chores around the house, and you shouldn't be too harsh on them if they are unable to take on the pressure. They will learn eventually as they grow up, as all children do, more or less.

Chapter 9: Talking about the Sensitive Issues in Life

Puberty comes early for children in this age, as early as when they are 9 or 10 years old. Their bodies change, yes; but that's not the most important changes that occur in your child. The way their thoughts and emotions change are more dramatic and noteworthy than the sudden changes in their physique. Even though children these days are more informed than we were, puberty is still a confusing time for them. And for the parents too!

Children grow up earlier these days. If you are thinking 9 or 10 is too early to talk about sensitive issues like puberty, dating or even sex, you are unfortunately wrong. By this time, they are already talking about these issues among their friends and getting confused by the minute. It is much better to hear all the right details from you.

Talking to Your Children About Puberty

You may think your child isn't conscious about their changing body, but they are. Even if they were a complete bookworm, a nerd, a geek or someone who lived in the clouds most of the times, your 9- to 11-year-old child is changing and they are definitely worried about their change. They might be smart enough to know where to look for answers, or they might be confused and looking at all the wrong places, but there's one thing for certain. No one can be a better teacher than you!

• **Puberty in Girls**

Girls react to their physical changes usually in two ways at this stage: either they are ashamed and humiliated by their figure, or they can't *wait to look as grown up as soon as possible.* Neither one is a healthy attitude to welcome puberty. There's nothing to be ashamed of developing breasts for girls, nor getting their periods, neither can this change be accelerated. This is what mothers need to talk to about with daughters who are on the verge of puberty, or who are going to start puberty very soon.

This can be a way to start a conversation to them:

> *"You must have noticed that you are growing up, haven't you? Yes, you're almost 10/11 and you're growing up very fast. And I don't just mean that you are so much taller than last year. You're a girl, just like me, and very soon you're going to start looking like me. A few more years and you're going to be just as tall as me, and look like me.*

> *"And do you know what else? As you are going to become a woman, it means that you are also going to develop your breasts. They're going to grow slowly, over the next few years, not immediately. No, they're not going to hurt, just like it doesn't hurt when you grow taller or when your hair grows. Your body is going to change because you are growing up, and your breasts will one day become like mine. And there's*

something else that you should also know now.

"Every month, all girls get their 'period' one time. It may scare you the first it happens, but I want you to know that this is not a disease. A period once a month is when we see blood coming out from our private part. This is nothing to worry about, because this happens to every other girl in the world. Yes, everyone. We may not talk about it but it happens to everyone, once every month. It will stay for three to five days, and then go away for the rest of the month. For some people, it can bring stomach ache, but nothing else. When this happens for you the first time, I will be there for you to help you with everything, so there's nothing for you to worry about. What you need to remember is, a period is completely natural and it happens to everyone. It's not a disease and you are not sick; it's just something that happens to us girls.

"Do you want to know why we get our periods...?"

You might want to postpone describing the reasons behind period until after your daughter is old enough to understand human biology. Usually, girls get their periods when they are 12 years old, so this talk is quite important around their 11th birthday. You need them to be ready for their first period when it comes so that the first signs of vaginal blood don't scare them. Even if they don't know why they are getting their periods, they should at least know to expect them.

Some girls can also get them as early as around when they are 10 years old, but there are some early signs of period. Girls get their periods around 2 years after their breasts start to develop, even slightly; and there's always going to be a slight trace of vaginal mucus in their panties before period starts for the first time. Start watching for these two signs to know if you need to have your "puberty talk" with your daughter soon.

- **<u>Puberty in Boys</u>**

In boys, it's all about growth. Puberty comes between 9 to 15 for boys, and they reach their final height within this time. Everything shoots up for them: their height, their limbs, their penis, their testes and their pubic hairs. They start to get facial hair and hair under their armpits, and their voices change and becomes deeper.

Boys aren't usually as embarrassed as some girls about the changes in their body; in fact, they start to notice girls more than they did before. One thing boys do hate is that some of them start to get really bad acne around puberty. This has something to do with their hormones and usually goes away before they enter their twenties.

The best person to talk to your sons about puberty is the father. But if you are close to your son, they might be more comfortable talking to their mother about their confusion, at least before they hit puberty. They don't need to know a lot of information regarding puberty, but they need to know that the changes they are experiencing in their bodies are normal.

Here's how you can talk to your son about puberty:

"You are growing up so fast! Have you noticed how you've grown taller suddenly these last few months? Why, you're almost my height. Do you know why you are suddenly spurting like this? Yes, you're almost 11, but it's something more than that. This age that you are in, it's called puberty. This means that this is a special time in your life when you are becoming a man.

"Everything is changing in your body. Your voice will be deeper from now on, and you are going to sound more like me. You are going to get hair everywhere: on your face, under your arms, on your chest, and around your private part.

"Speaking of your private part, have you noticed any change around it? It's going to get bigger too, and that's not only because you are growing taller. It's because you are growing into a man."

Your child might start getting embarrassed at this point of the conversation and quickly change the subject. However, it is important for them to know exactly what a penis does before they find the answers from pornographic sites. If you are not comfortable in explaining about sex, you can give them reliable books to read, instead of letting them search for inappropriate content on Google. You can also postpone the discussion of sex for a few years until you see them show interest in girls and dating.

Talking to Your Children About Responsibility

When they are young, children usually don't have any idea about where their food, clothing and other belongings come from. They aren't born with the concept of money or what goes on behind the transactions that take place over the shop counters. However, this is the age when children should be taught about economic responsibility. They don't need to be responsible for their own meals or basic needs, but they should know a fraction of what effort it takes their parents to earn the money that puts food on their table.

It's a good idea to give them paid jobs at this age, or a pocket money they'll get only if they complete their chores for the week. In this way, they won't have to do a whole lot much every day that will hamper their daily routine, but they'll get the satisfaction of getting paid for them. Just like their parents, they'll be earning their privileges at home. If they want some extra money for themselves, they can earn by doing extra chores. This will teach them to be responsible with money, because they'll learn to spend what they have earned themselves.

Talking to Your Children About Peer Pressure

Another form of responsibility is to know what's good for them, instead of succumbing to peer pressure. This is a mistake many kids make in their puberty; they listen to other children they think are their "friends" and try smoking, drugs or bullying. These are bad choices they make that might seriously affect their life, even in the future. Kids, at this stage, are heavily influenced by their peers; unfortunately, they listen more to their friends and classmates than to their conscience or their parents.

This is something definitely worth talking to your pre-teen about. Here's how you can try:

> *"You're growing up fast, my love. I'm not going to tell you what to do for when you are older; you'll have to use your own brains to decide your action. There will be a lot of options in front of you to choose from, but you have to only choose the right one. If your friends tease someone, should you do it too? What would you do if they are doing something you don't want to? What would you do if they start smoking? Would you do it too?*
>
> *"Growing up doesn't mean you can do anything you want to do. It means you know in your heart the right thing to do. You'll know you're growing up when you know the right thing to do. Growing up means knowing to be responsible. You can be responsible when you can control yourself to do what's right, and not what others are doing."*

If this is too complicated for them to understand, you can empathize with them a little more.

> *"Does it ever happen that you don't like something that your friends are doing, but you end up doing it anyway just so that you won't stand out? Did they smoke or try drugs, but you didn't want to? Did they bully*

someone and you were forced you to join? Did they tease someone and you really hated that? This is because you are growing up now. And you are growing a mind of your own. Your mind will tell you what's the right thing to do and what's wrong.

*"When you are a grown up, it means that you can do anything you want to. But you should only do what you think is right. Doing what others are telling you **but you don't like means giving in to peer pressure, and that's not right.** You don't have to do what your friends are asking you to do if you don't think it is right for you.*

*"The friends who will force you to behave like them, knowing you are not comfortable, aren't true friends. Real friends will understand what you want and they'll never force you. **If the people you call your friends are forcing you to smoke, or try drugs, or be a bully, or anything you don't want to do, you should think again if you want to be friends with them.**"*

Ultimately, it'll be their own decision. After they reach a certain age, you can't really force your children to do anything against their wishes. You can command them, ground them or punish them, but they will do what they want. It is better, especially in the long run, to help them develop their own conscience so that they know what to do in confusing situations.

Talking to Your Children About Sex

Many parents talk about sex as the main reason behind having children, as an answer to the question "Where do babies come from?" While this is, of course, one of the main reasons behind sexual intercourse between a man and a woman, it's not the only one.

Still, when your children are 10 or 11 years old, they have already witnessed a number of sex scenes on TV, and may have probably looked at pornographic sites/pictures as well. They will get an unhealthy idea about sex if you don't explain the facts to them. Explaining about sex isn't easy for a parent, no matter how composed you are. It will be embarrassed for both you and your child to talk about something that is both sensitive, private and embarrassing.

You might start by asking what they know about sex. They might know the process, but the reasons and the motives behind it may be foreign to them. More importantly, they can't even imagine their parents ever having sex, not the way they've seen it on TV and on YouTube. You need to explain the reasons behind having sex more than the procedure of it.

Here's how you can try talking about it:

> *"You're growing up and very soon, you are going to start noticing someone you like. When you find a girl/guy you like, you would want to start dating, and since you are old enough, I wouldn't stop you. Of course you should go on a date with the*

person you like, get to know them, kiss them and get intimate with them. This is a part of growing up.

"Sex ultimately becomes an agenda when you are dating someone. You might want to have sex with someone you are dating, but be absolutely sure you are ready for this. Your first time comes only once in your life and you'd want it to be with someone special. Don't have sex because everyone else is having it, but because you are sure. Wait until you love someone enough to let them be the first one; it doesn't have to be the person you've decided to spend your whole life with, but it should be someone you'd want to remember all your life."

You can postpone the sex talk until your child is at least 14 or 15 but some children become sexually active even before that age. It's hard for parents to imagine their preteen child having sex with someone, but it happens in a lot of cases, mainly before they are ready. But what your children need to hear from you is that having sex doesn't mean the end of the world, and that the most important factor is to keep themselves safe. This is especially important for girls, as they are the ones who can end up pregnant as early as 14, and change the course of their whole life.

"I'd rather you wait a little while before you have sex, because you have your whole life ahead of you for that. These years that you are spending now are the last years of your childhood, and you're going to miss them

later. Sex is going to make you grow up faster than you were naturally meant to, but that's okay. If you are seeing someone and if you are serious about someone, I can't stop you from getting sexually involved with them.

"What's most important now is that you should both keep yourself safe. Use protection; practice safe sex. You are very, very young and a pregnancy can ruin everything for you now. Having sex isn't the worst thing that you can do now, but having unprotected sex is. Be responsible in your actions, because you have your whole life ahead of you."

Most importantly, your child should know that they can always come to you for rational advice and non-judgemental help. If they do end up making a mistake, they should have you as a backup plan for help. If they are afraid of you or if they know you are going to penalize them for their mistake, they might end up taking drastic measures themselves. A lot of pregnant teenager damage their bodies severely or even kill themselves trying to get an illegal abortion or in fear of their parents. You certainly don't want your children trying something like that, do you?

Preteen is a difficult time for children; they are growing up, but not yet grown up, neither are they children anymore. This is a special age that needs understanding and rationalization more than it needs discipline and rules, and the parents are the perfect people for it.

Chapter 10: "Do you know your Teen?"

Teenagers can be moody, surly, distant and sometimes, disrespectful. Getting information out of them is harder. They can stare at their phone for hours but won't look at your for even a second. They'll giggle and chat with their friends the whole day, but refuse to answer a straight query from you. You'll miss the clingy two-year old who wouldn't leave you alone for five minutes to let you go to the toilet in peace or the five-year-old who'd talk and talk, and make you crazy.

But there are some things that you need to always know about your teenagers, always, even if you have to ask them a thousand times. Tactfully, of course. This is the time to notice more than you ask them directly. If they don't want to answer your questions directly, you need to notice their actions so that you know exactly what they are up to. This isn't invasion of privacy, no! As the parent, this is a part of your job. At this age, you need to know the type of person your child is growing up to become.

Do you know the answers to these questions?

(The following pages are printable. You can print this page below and write down the answers. The answers will tell you if you are paying enough attention to your teenage children.)

Who are their best friend(s)?

_____

____

Are they sure about/comfortable with their sexual
orientation? _____

Who is their girl/boyfriend?

_____

____

Is there something they are passionate about?

_____

Do they read?

_____

_____

Name one book/the last book you've seen them read.

_____

_____

_____

What kind of music do they listen to?

_____

_____

_____

What TV series/movie franchise are they passionate about? _____

_____

_____

What sports (if any) do they watch/play?

_____

What instrument (if any) do they play?

_____

Do they collect anything?

_____

_____

What is their favorite subject at school?

_____

Who is their favorite teacher?

_____

___

Did they ever have a crush on someone?

_____

Is there any political leader they admire?

_____

Who is their favorite historical character?

_____

Where is their favorite after school hangout?

_____

Do they smoke?

_____

_____

Have they ever tried drugs?

_____

_____

Are they sexually active?

_____

_____

Are they using protection (if sexually active)?

_____

Do they have more than one sexual partners at one
time? _____

Have they ever gotten into any trouble in school?

_____

Is there anyone is school they don't get along with?

_____

Do they collect anything?

_____

_____

Have they ever bullied someone?

_____

Have they ever been bullied?

_____
____

What have they been bullied (if they have been) about?

_____

_____

_____

Do they like school?

_____

_____

How much time do they spend outdoors?

_____

How much time do they spend on the Internet?

_____

How much time do they spend on their phone?

_____

How much time do they spend behind locked doors in their room? _____

Do they sleep well at night?

_____

_____

Do they have a healthy appetite?

_____

Do they eat too much junk food?

_____

Are they secretive/Do they have a secret?

_____

Do they write in a journal?

_____

_____

Do they have an outlet for their creativity/anger?

_____

Who do they talk to when
angry/frustrated/disappointed/sad?

_____

Who do they talk to when happy/excited?

_____

Which has been their favorite vacation so far?

_____

What is their dream vacation destination?

_____

Have they set a goal for their future profession yet?

_____

What had been their dream to become as a child?

_____

Has your profession influenced their decision in any way? _____

Is their professional choice a result of your decision?

_____

Is their future profession of choice something they are passionate about? _____

Has your profession influenced their decision in any way? _____

Have they ever shown signs of depression?

_____

Do they sleep for long hours sometimes?

_____

Have they shown signs of hurting/cutting themselves?

_____

Are they always or often disrespectful of you?

_____

Are they cordial with your extended family?

_____

Do they have a favorite
cousin/uncle/grandparent/aunt?

_____

Chapter 11: Understanding Teenage Problems and Offering Solutions

Teenage problems are many these days, and much more complicated than what we parents used to face in our time. Our children, lucky in a lot of ways, also face a lot more problem in their lives. Unfortunately, not everyone is strong enough to face these troubles; very often, they end up making wrong choices in their lives, choices that will affect the rest of their lives.

Dropouts, unprotected sex and experiments with drugs – these are the worst decisions that these troubled teenagers make in this confusing time of their lives. They can also have mental breakdowns because of bullying, develop various types of mental disorders or even suffer from eating disorders at this time of their life. It is up to the parents to help these teenagers at this stage, even though they will not ask for help or even resist any kind of help.

Understand their Problems

The first thing you need to do is to understand the troubles they are going through. As you are the adult and they are the emotional ones in the relationship, your point of views will, of course, not match. **We've seen life more than they have and their problems might seem extremely trifle to us, but they are monumental to them.** For a teenager, it is more important to feel accepted in high school than to think about everything that is going wrong in the world.

First of all, to understand your teenage child, you need to know the common problems of this particular age:

- **Improper body Image.** Thanks to the unhealthy body image portrayed in our media, all girls think they need to have a zero-sized body to be considered beautiful. This paves the way for eating disorders like anorexia and bulimia, etc.

- **Social Pressure.** Because everyone has to be popular. Everyone has to be special and talented.

- **Parental Pressure.** When kids put pressure on themselves to be just as talented and special as their parents believe they are, often exhausting themselves in the process.

- **Drugs and Alcohol.** So-called friends daring and taunting teenagers to experiment in drugs and drinking, even if they don't want to. Drinking socially to fit in; trying drugs to be accepted into the popular group.

- **Underage, unprotected sex.** Raging hormones in boys emotionally blackmailing or forcing girls to have sex with them, sometimes resulting in pregnancies or STDs. Most girls usually agree to sex despite not being ready because they don't want their popular boyfriends to break up with them, as there are other girls ready to have sex.

- **Bullying.** Kids today are being bullied for everything, from being too smart to being too tall. They get bullied if they read a lot or if they have a large vocabulary. If they dare to do anything different or be a little different, or don't want to be popular, they are bullied by the kids that are considered to be the popular ones in high school.

- **Cyber Bullying.** If your kids are not being bullied directly, they can also be bullied online. Bullies hide behind anonymous personas to call others names or threat them online.

- **Depression.** This is more of a symptom than a reason, but a lot of teenagers these days are suffering from depression. The reason could be anything, or more than one; but this is a difficult age where the problems are many and the capability to deal with them limited.

Talking to your Teenager

As an adult, it is very hard to understand what your teenager is going through, as some of their biggest concerns might seem unnecessary and frivolous to you. You have gone past the age of caring about being accepted by your peers and you are probably okay with your body, but these are the main anxieties of a teenager.

Talking to them could be harder. If you don't understand their worries, you might end up exclaiming *"But that's nothing to be worried about!"* to something that's bothering them, and this will shut them off for good. If they comprehend that you are not at all being serious about what's actually a huge deal with them, they will stop communicating with you completely.

To talk to your teenager, you have to stop thinking like the adult that you are, and remember the teenager that you once were. Once when you were their age, your worries and self-doubts must have seen pointless to an adult, but they were immense to you. This is how it is for your child now.

So, talk to them like you understand.

- Be honest about your own high school experience. Were you bullied in high school? What did that make you feel? Did you feel guilty (if you were a bully) about being mean to your classmates? Why did you think you were a bully? Were you unhappy? Did being a bully make you feel powerful? Do you think you'd do it differently if you knew better? Or (if you were bullied) did you ever want to drop out because you couldn't take it anymore? What would you say to your bully if you could see them now? Do you know what they are doing these days? Are they doing better than you, or worst?

- Did you have "friends" who wanted you to try something risky, like drugs or risky? Did you ever drink and drive? Or do anything dangerous because of them? Did it affect your life? Do you think they were your real friends if they goaded you to dangerous activities? Would you be friends with them now? Do you regret your actions now?

- [For women mostly] Did you have sex with your high school boyfriend because he was pressuring you, before you were ready? Do you wish you'd said 'no'? Do you wish it was with someone more special, someone you wouldn't regret later? Did you have sex so that your boyfriend wouldn't break up with you? Do you wish you could have waited a little later?

- [For women] Did you waste hours in high school trying to look your best? Did you stop eating so that you could be thinner and prettier? Did you think you were fat even though you were actually the right size? Was your body image constantly on your mind? Instead of having fun with friends, did you constantly fret about eating too much, gaining too much weight, not being pretty enough?

Don't start preaching your teenage child; don't make them sit down in front of you and give them a lecture. They are past the age of a lecture. They need a friend more than they need a fretting parent at this age. Tell them stories of your teenage; they might be interested. Don't make it sound like advice on how to live their life. Make it sound like just what it is: a story from your youth.

"Did I ever tell you about this guy I went to high school with? His name was John. I suddenly came across his profile on Facebook the other day, and I remembered him. Boy, has he changed from high school. He was one of the worst bullies you have ever seen. I was his biggest target...."

"This girl reminds me of someone (While watching a movie with your child). I used to go to high school with this girl, Jane. But she was so pretty, and smart too. So smart, and probably the most bullied girl in the

*whole school, just because she was both
smart and pretty."*

That's how you should do it. Don't give them the half-hearted assurance that everything will be all right, show them. Compare your own life to what it was in high school, or with the other people who went to school with you. If they are being bullied, show them the people who had been bullied and are now risen to the top of the field.

Most importantly, show them that life doesn't end in high school. Actually, real life begins after high school. High school and teenage is tough, but it just prepares them for the later part of their life. Life will get better from there on. If they can survive high school with their heads held high, they can achieve anything in life.

Conclusion

Be a Positive Parent to have a Positive Child

It all comes down to this: be positive. Be confident in your ability as a parent and you will be a good parent. If you are overwhelmed and overemphasized, you will only end up stressed and harassed. Parenting is hard, and don't let anyone tell you otherwise. Being a good parent is the hardest job you have to do in your life, much harder than anything else. It will anger you, drain you, stress you and irritate you, but at the end of the day, it's worth it.

Don't yell at your children – that's Rule#1.

Be patient – that's Rule#2.

Be Positive – that's Rule#3.

The rest you can figure out on yourself. By book "Stop Yelling and Love Me More, Please Mom! Workbook" is both for the mothers and the children, an answer to all the cries for help I've heard in unhappy and stressful homes. I've tried my best to give answers to being the best parent you can (within reason) to your child, and to maintain an air of positive welfare in your home. Not all children are the same, and not all mothers are the same. Some mothers have less patience than others, but they can be patient and positive mothers too if they try.

All the best!

That's what I'm here trying to figure out. How am I reacting to everything between us being over?

"I'm not as happy as I should be, if I'm being honest." I look up from where I'd been staring at my feet.

He cocks his head to the side and studies me, opening his mouth to say something, then closing it. He steps closer to me, dusting himself off.

"Why is that?" he asks when he's in my airspace. My breath hitches, and any words I had disappear.

He lifts my chin with his forefinger, forcing me to look into his eyes. "Why is that?" he repeats.

"Because I'm in love with you." It just comes out, but now that it's in the universe, it feels right. I don't know how long I've been in love with him, but the feeling overwhelms me now. A laugh bubbles out of me. That's why this didn't feel right. I've been faking what's been real this whole time. We worked to get to know each other to make everything look real, and what we really did was make it real.

"Finally. Fucking finally!" he exclaims as he grabs me around my waist and swings me in the air. He sets me down carefully, then he gets down on one knee.

"What are you doing?" I squeal.

He takes my hand. "I'm doing it right. I really want to marry you and build a real future with you, have babies with you, and be myself forever with you. Charisse Turner, will you really marry me?"

I kneel down with him and take his face into my hands. "Of

course I will marry you, Dru," I tell him before we kiss.

Epilogue

The morning sun kisses the garden, turning everything it touches into gold. I stand at the entrance, my heart fluttering like the delicate wings of the butterflies flitting around the blooming flowers. Everyone I love stands at the end of the aisle. Today, in front of the world, I marry Dru, the man who turned my world upside down, in the best way possible.

I smooth down my dress, a sleek, modern creation that feels like a second skin. It's perfect—just like this day promises to be. Porsche and Lily stand looking like beauty queens. I had no involvement in their dress buying. Dru put them on a plane with an unlimited budget, and they absolutely understood the assignment.

Taking a deep breath, I step forward into the next chapter of my life. My gaze locks on Dru. He stands at the altar, looking like he stepped out of a dream, in his custom suit with a razor sharp hairline. His eyes brim with emotions. This has been an interesting journey. It's hard to believe we've made it.

As I walk down the aisle, I catch glimpses of our friends and family. Draymond and Drummond are here, their twin presence a comforting reminder of the bond Dru shares with them. They're laughing about something, their heads close together —a moment I know Dru will cherish. I hope one of the photographers catches that.

Porsche and Lily are side by side with Dreya, ever the picture of sophistication, standing beside them. My relationship with my sister may still be broken, but these three women are my chosen family.

Reaching the altar, Dru takes my hands in his, and his touch sends a wave of warmth through me. "You look stunning," he whispers, and I can only smile in response.

Everything is a blur until Dru begins his vows. His hands are warm and steady, a testament to how he feels about what we're doing. There's not a nervous bone in his body right now.

"Charisse, from the moment I met you, my world shifted on its axis. You came into my life like a whirlwind, challenging me, inspiring me, and showing me what it truly means to love and be loved. Today, as I stand before you, I am overwhelmed with gratitude and love.

"In your eyes, I see a future filled with laughter, passion, and endless possibilities. In your smile, I find the warmth and comfort of home. And in your heart, I've discovered a love so profound, it transcends everything I ever imagined.

"I vow to be your partner in every sense of the word. To stand by you through the highs and the lows, the triumphs and the challenges. I promise to listen to you, to learn from you, and to grow with you, day by day.

"I vow to cherish the quirks that make you uniquely you, to celebrate your strengths, and to offer my shoulder for the moments when you feel weak. I will be your confidant, your co-conspirator, and your closest friend.

"I promise to keep our lives exciting, adventurous, and full of passion. To support your dreams and to walk beside you as we build our future together.

"And above all, I vow to be true to you, to respect you, and to shower you with all the love I have, for all the days of my life.

"Charisse, you are my heart, my soul, my everything. Today, I give you my hand, my heart, and my promise, that no matter where life takes us, I will always be there, loving you more and more with each passing day."

I'm fighting back tears, and I take a shaky breath before I say my own.

"Dru, when I first met you, I never imagined that this day would come. Our beginning was like a dance, one where I was convinced I knew all the steps, yet you came along and changed the rhythm entirely. My friends saw it before I did — they saw how you'd come to mean the world to me. And me? I spent far too long denying the truth that was as clear as day: I had fallen for you, completely and irrevocably.

"I vow to be your partner, your confidante, your pillar of strength in every challenge we face. In you, I've found a love that is both a sanctuary and a spark, a love that inspires and comforts.

"I promise to cherish every moment with you, from the quiet mornings to the starry nights. To stand beside you, to dream with you, and to build a future that's brighter because we're together.

"I vow to keep our love alive, to nurture it with kindness, understanding, and patience. To remember that even on the difficult days, what we have is rare and beautiful.

"I promise to listen to you with an open heart, to speak words of love and encouragement, and to always be the one you can lean on. My love for you is a journey, starting at forever and ending at never.

"Dru, you are my unexpected love, my greatest adventure, and my eternal comfort. Today, in front of our families, our friends

who knew all along, and the world, I give you my hand, my heart, and my promise. A promise to love you more deeply with each passing day, in every chapter of the beautiful story we are writing together."

We seal our vows with a kiss. We'd agreed on a little peck, but Dru takes my face into his hands and brings his lips to mine like I'm water, and he's a man lost at sea. He drinks me in, caressing my cheek as his tongue glides across mine. He bites my bottom lip, making me moan quietly.

"They're watching," I say into Dru's mouth as he extends the kiss for much longer than anticipated. "You're going to make me want to leave before we get to the reception."

He pulls away. "You're my wife now. We're going to do what husbands and wives do—right now, and definitely later." He kisses me again and grabs my ass, causing the crowd to erupt in cheers and applause.

The reception is a whirlwind of music, laughter, and dancing. I find myself swept into conversations with everyone, feeling like the happiest person alive.

Porsche scoffs at me after catching the bouquet. "You set this up. I don't want this!" she teases, her laugh infectious. She holds the bouquet to her heart and dances with it. Lily stands beside her laughing.

Draymond and Drummond stand at the microphone to give the Best Man's toast. Dru hangs his head knowing the nonsense they're about to spew. I nudge him and smile. His brothers love him so much.

"Dru," Draymond begins, "How did you manage to pull someone like Charisse?"

"He flashed his money because we know he has no game," Draymond answers, making Dru's face fall.

I stand up and feign offense with my hands on my hips at the idea of being bought, then I glance at Dru and wink. This is going to be our inside joke throughout our whole marriage. The crowd roars with laughter, and eventually Dru joins in.

"But for real, Dru, we love you and we're happy for you. Charisse, we come as a package deal, so it's nice to have two sisters now. You fit in and match the energy so well. We're happy to have you in the family," Draymond finishes.

I stand up and blow kisses at both of them, mouthing "Thank you" and putting my hand to my heart. I'm joining a family that embraces me completely, and it's everything I never knew I needed.

Dru and I steal a moment together over our meal, our fingers entwined. "We did it," he says, his voice thick with emotion.

"We did," I agree, leaning into him. "We can keep this contract signed though."

He bursts out laughing and holds his drink up to me. "We can definitely drink to that!"

As the night draws to a close, Dru and I share our final dance under the stars. The world falls away until it's just the two of us, moving to a rhythm that's ours alone.

"We're starting a new chapter," I say, my head resting on his shoulder and imagining the life I never thought I'd have with the love I didn't think I deserved.

"A beautiful, endless chapter," Dru agrees, and I know he's right.

The End

Books In This Series

The Martin Brothers

Dru, Draymond, and Drummond Martin have the money, the looks, and the swag, but they don't have the women who make their lives complete.

Love, Under Contract

Love, From Scratch

Coming in April!

Love, Undercover

Made in the USA
Monee, IL
21 July 2024

62191954R00138

Made in the USA
Monee, IL
23 September 2021